This edition published by Concordia Publishing House
3558 South Jefferson Avenue, St. Louis, MO 63118-3968
1-800-325-3040 • www.cph.org

ISBN 10: 0-7586-1634-1
ISBN 13: 978-0-7586-1634-0

Printed in China.

10 9 8 7 6 5 4 3 2 1 17 16 15 14 13 12 11 10 09 08

CHILDREN'S BIBLE STORIES

As told by Dana Forrest Kennedy
Illustrated by Ellen Dolce

Concordia Publishing House • Saint Louis

The Old Testament

The New Testament

Introduction

❧

The Bible is the most important book ever written. It tells stories about people—their lives, their hopes, their thoughts. But what makes the Bible important is that it is the Word of God. In it, God reveals who He is, what He does, and how He wants to be involved in our lives.

This children's Bible is a selection of favorite stories told in a way that not only brings them vividly to life for young children, but also encourages them to read the Bible for themselves as they grow older.

This book shares the wondrous truth that God created us, loves us, forgives us, and, through His Son, Jesus Christ, provides us with the means of salvation.

To God be the glory!

The Old Testament

God Made Everything

In the beginning, God created the heavens and the earth.
The earth was without form and void, and darkness was over the face of the deep.
Genesis 1:1–2

In the beginning, the universe was dark and shapeless and empty. There were no animals, no birds, no people, no blue sky, no earth, no sun.

God created the earth with oceans and dry land. He made the sun to give light during the day and the stars to shine at night. God filled the oceans with fishes and the dry land with plants and animals.

Last of all, God made Adam and Eve. He made them in His image, which is holy. And He gave them the beautiful Garden of Eden.

God saw that everything He made was good.

"Everything in this garden is yours," God said to them, "except the tree of knowledge. You must not eat its fruit."

But the evil one entered the garden in the form of a snake. He tempted Eve saying, "Eat the fruit. It won't hurt you. It will make you wise like God."

So Eve ate the fruit. Then she gave some to Adam, and he ate it, too.

God was sad and angry that Adam and Eve had disobeyed Him. He sent them out of the Garden of Eden. Then God placed an angel with a flaming sword to guard the entrance to the garden so they could never return.

But God did something else. He promised Adam and Eve that one day He would send a Savior to His people.

An Angry Brother

*When they were in the field,
Cain rose up against his brother Abel and killed him.*
Genesis 4:8

$\mathcal{A}$dam and Eve had two sons, Cain and Abel. Cain was a farmer and Abel was a shepherd. One day Cain and Abel both brought offerings to God. Abel's gift pleased God more than Cain's.

This made Cain angry. He found Abel alone in a field and killed him.

Later God asked Cain, "Where is your brother?"

Cain answered, "I don't know. Am I my brother's keeper?"

"The ground cries out that you killed your brother," God said. "You have done a terrible thing."

So God punished Cain. He told him that he had to leave his home and wander all over the world. No crops would grow for him, and everyone would know of his sin.

Cain was afraid someone would try to kill him. But God put a special mark on Cain's forehead so no one would harm him. Cain would have to live with his punishment.

Noah's Big Boat

Only Noah was left, and those who were with him in the ark.
Genesis 7:23

As time passed, God looked at the world He had made and saw that people had become wicked and evil. There was only one man, Noah, who was faithful and good and loved God. One day God said to Noah, "I am going to start again. I will flood the earth with water and destroy every living creature. But, first, I want you to build a big strong boat, an ark.

"Then take two of every kind of animal and bird into the ark. Take two elephants, two monkeys, two leopards, two rabbits, and two ducks—two of every animal, bird, and insect in the world. Take all your family and all the creatures into your ark. There you will be safe."

Noah did as God told him. Then it began to rain. It rained for 40 days and 40 nights.

Water covered the whole world, but Noah's big boat floated on top of the flood waters. At last the rain stopped. The water began to go down. Noah sent out a dove to see if any dry land had appeared. The dove returned with an olive branch in her beak, so Noah knew the earth was drying up and they would soon be able to leave the ark.

When the ark came to rest on top of a mountain, God told Noah he could now take his family off the big boat. So Noah and his family walked onto the dry land with all the animals and birds following after them.

Noah made an altar and worshipped God, thanking Him for saving their lives and for the return of dry land.

God was happy with Noah and put a beautiful rainbow in the sky to show His pleasure.

"This is a sign of My love and faithfulness," God said. "I promise I will never flood the earth again."

Abraham's Terrible Test

*Abraham built the altar there and laid the wood in order
and bound Isaac his son and laid him on the altar, on top of the wood.*
Genesis 22:9

*O*nce again, people filled the earth, and among them
there was a good man called Abraham. God chose him
for a special plan. He promised Abraham He would bless
him and make a great nation from Abraham's family.

Then God gave a son to Abraham and his wife,
Sarah. They named him Isaac.

One day God called to Abraham, "Abraham, take
Isaac, your only son, whom you love so much. Go into
the wilderness and sacrifice him to Me."

Usually Abraham would sacrifice a lamb and offer it to God. Must he sacrifice his son this time? This made Abraham very sad, but he knew he must obey God. The next morning Abraham loaded his donkey and set out with Isaac.

Isaac did not understand what was happening. "Where is the lamb that we are going to sacrifice?" he asked his father.

Abraham replied, "God will give us one."

Then Abraham built an altar. He put Isaac on top of the altar. Slowly, he took out his knife.

Just then a voice from heaven called out, "Stop! Don't hurt the boy. I now know you love Me because you obeyed My voice."

Just then Abraham saw a ram caught in the nearby bushes.

Instead of his son, Abraham sacrificed the ram and offered it to God. God was pleased.

Rebekah at the Well

Behold, Rebekah came out with her water jar on her shoulder.
Genesis 24:45

Abraham was growing old, and before he died he wanted to find the right wife for his son, Isaac. So he sent a trusted servant back to the place where he had come from. Abraham believed that God would help his servant find a wife for Isaac.

When the servant came to the town, he went to its well where women came to get water. He prayed to God that the first woman who gave water to him and his animals be the one Isaac should marry. Soon, the beautiful Rebekah came to the well with her pitcher on her shoulder.

The servant asked Rebekah for a drink. She not only gave him water, but also brought some for his animals. He knew this was God's sign.

The servant then asked Rebekah's family if she could go back with him to marry Isaac. "Yes," they said. "This is what God wants." The servant was so thankful that he bowed down and praised God.

Then Rebekah went back with the servant to Isaac's home. She became Isaac's wife and he loved her.

Joseph's Coat of Many Colors

[Jacob] loved Joseph more than any other of his sons …
he made him a robe of many colors.
Genesis 37:3

*A*fter Isaac and Rebekah married, they had a son
named Jacob. When Jacob grew up, he had twelve
sons. He loved them all, but he loved Joseph the most.
He made Joseph a beautiful coat of many colors. The
gift made Joseph's brothers jealous and angry.

One day Jacob sent Joseph out to visit his brothers, who were working in the fields far from home. When Joseph found his brothers, they took his beautiful coat from him and sold him to a band of traders who were going to Egypt.

Then the brothers dipped Joseph's coat in goat's blood and took it home to show their father.

"It is Joseph's coat," Jacob said. "He must have been killed by wild animals." Jacob was very sad. He did not know that his son was still alive and that they would be reunited someday.

Pharaoh's Mysterious Dreams

*And Pharaoh said to Joseph, "I have had a dream…
I have heard it said of you that when you hear a dream you can interpret it."*
Genesis 41:15

The traders took Joseph with them into Egypt, where they sold him again. Later he was thrown in jail with Pharaoh's servant and baker. Both men had mysterious dreams that God helped Joseph to explain. When the servant was released from prison, Joseph said, "Tell Pharaoh about me, and help me get free."

Sometime later, Pharaoh had two strange dreams. The servant told Pharaoh about Joseph, and Pharaoh sent for him.

"I have dreamed that seven fat cows were eaten up by seven lean ones," Pharaoh said. "Then I dreamed that seven plump stalks of grain were eaten up by seven thin stalks. Can you tell me what this means?"

"There will be seven years of plenty followed by seven years of famine," Joseph said. "Egypt must prepare."

Pharaoh was so impressed with Joseph's wisdom that he made him the keeper of Egypt's grain.

Sure enough, after seven years of plenty there came a great famine. Joseph's brothers became so hungry that they came to Egypt to buy food from Pharaoh's grain keeper.

When Joseph told them who he was, his brothers were afraid. They thought he would still be angry and would punish them for selling him long ago, but Joseph had forgiven them.

"Don't be afraid," Joseph told his brothers. "God sent me into Egypt to save lives." Joseph embraced his brothers and gave them food. Soon he brought his father and all his brothers to Egypt to live with him.

Moses Among the Bulrushes

She took for him a basket made of bulrushes. . . .
She put the child in it and placed it among the reeds by the river bank.
Exodus 2:3

Moses was a beautiful baby boy. His parents were descendants of Abraham, Isaac, and Jacob. They were called the children of Israel and they were living in Egypt. A wicked pharaoh did not like the children of Israel. He forced them to be slaves and wanted all their boy babies killed. Moses' mother had a plan to save her son. She put him in a basket among the bulrushes at the river's edge.

Moses' sister, Miriam, stood in the rushes to watch the basket. Soon it floated near the king's daughter, who came to the river to bathe. She heard the baby crying and peered into the bulrushes. There was little Moses in the basket.

"He is an Israelite baby," she said. "I must save him. I will keep him for my own."

"Would you like me to find someone to nurse the baby for you?" asked Miriam.

"Yes," the princess said.

So Miriam brought the baby home to their mother who took care of him. When Moses was old enough, he went to live at the princess's house and became her son. Although Moses was not with his own people, God never stopped watching over him. God always watches over us, too.

An Amazing Fire

And Moses said, "I will turn aside to
see this great sight, why the bush is not burned."
Exodus 3:3

One day, as Moses was leading his flock of sheep along the side of a mountain, he came upon a bush that was on fire. Moses went closer and saw a strange sight. The bush was not being consumed by the flames!

"Take off your shoes," said a voice from the burning bush. "You are on holy ground."

"Who speaks?" asked Moses.

"I am the God of Abraham," the voice answered. "I want you to go to Pharaoh and tell him to let the children of Israel go free."

"I can't do that," said Moses. "Pharaoh won't listen to me."

"You can do it with My help," said God. "You will use your shepherd's staff to show Pharaoh that I have sent you. Throw your staff on the ground."

Moses followed God's instructions. When he threw down the staff, it turned into a snake. When he picked it up, it became a staff again.

Moses knew that God would help him, so he set off for Egypt to ask Pharaoh to let his people go.

The Great Escape

*The waters were divided. And the people of Israel went
into the midst of the sea on dry ground, the waters being
a wall to them on their right hand and on their left.*
Exodus 14:21–22

With God's help, Moses tried many things to help his
people escape from Egypt. But Pharaoh would not let the
children of Israel go. He wanted to keep them as his slaves.

Finally, God said to Moses, "I will do one more thing,
then Pharaoh will let My people go. Have the people paint
lamb's blood over their doors tonight. Every house marked
this way will be safe. Tell them to pack their things, eat a
quick supper, and be ready to leave in a hurry."

At midnight the children of Israel heard a loud crying coming from the homes of the Egyptians. The oldest son in every Egyptian home was dead, even Pharaoh's son. But the sons of the Israelites were spared. Pharaoh finally decided to let the children of Israel go.

But they had not gone far when Pharaoh changed his mind. He chased after them with soldiers in chariots pulled by fast horses.

The children of Israel ran until they came to the Red Sea. With the enemy behind them and no way to cross the sea, they were trapped!

"Stand firm," said Moses, "and see how God will help you." Moses stretched out his hand over the sea, and God pushed the water out of the way so they could cross on dry ground.

The children of Israel walked on a dry path through the sea. But when the Egyptians followed, the walls of water fell in on Pharaoh, the soldiers, and their horses and drowned them. At last the children of Israel were free. God had saved them just as He had said He would!

Rules from Above

The LORD said to Moses, "Write these words. . . ."
And he wrote on the tablets the words of the covenant,
the Ten Commandments.
Exodus 34:27–28

*A*fter the children of Israel had wandered in the
desert for many days, they came to a high mountain.

God told Moses to climb the mountain, and there He
gave him ten laws carved into two stone tablets. "These
are My Commandments," God said to Moses. "I want all
My people to obey them."

Moses took the tablets and went back down the mountain. There he found the children of Israel worshipping a golden statue of a calf instead of worshipping the true God. In a rage, Moses threw down the stone tablets, and they broke into pieces.

When the people realized that worshiping an idol was wrong, they were sorry. Moses said he would ask God to forgive them. Moses went back up the mountain, where God again wrote His Laws on two new stones.

"Keep My Commandments," said God, "and I will give you a new land."

When Moses came down from the mountain, his face glowed. He gave the people the new tablets and told them always to follow God's Laws. These are the Commandments we still learn and follow today.

The Walls That Fell Down

*As soon as the people heard the sound of the trumpet, the people shouted
a great shout, and the wall fell down flat.*
Joshua 6:20

After Moses died, God chose Joshua to lead the
children of Israel into the land of Canaan, which He had
promised them. Two things stood in their way, the
Jordan River and the city of Jericho.

At the Jordan River, Joshua told the priests carrying
the Ark—the special box containing the stone tablets—
to lead their people into the river. As soon as the
priests' feet touched the water, God drew the river back
so the children of Israel could walk across on dry land.

Then they had to face the soldiers of Jericho.

"Joshua," God said, "march your people around the city walls for seven days. Carry the Ark with you. On the seventh day, have the priests blow one long note on their horns. At the same time, have everyone give a loud shout."

The children of Israel did what Joshua told them to
do. On the seventh day, when the priests blew their
horns, the people gave a loud shout, and the walls of
Jericho came tumbling down! The city was theirs!

How Gideon Beat the Enemy

And they blew the trumpets and smashed the jars. . .
and they cried out, "A sword for the LORD and for Gideon."
Judges 7:19, 20

For many years the children of Israel had been ruled by the Midianites.

One day, as Gideon was working in his father's fields, an angel came to him and said, "The Lord is with you and He will help you defeat the Midianites."

Gideon selected an army of 300 men. They planned to trick the Midianites during an attack at night. Each Israelite soldier carried a light covered by a pitcher in his left hand and a trumpet in his right hand. When the time came, Gideon and all his soldiers blew their trumpets and broke their pitchers, letting their lights shine. Then they all shouted loudly, "For the Lord and for Gideon!"

Scared by the noise and the light, the Midianites ran in every direction. Gideon and his soldiers chased them right out of the country.

"Gideon, be our king," the children of Israel begged.

"No," replied Gideon. "God will be your King!
Obey Him."

So, the Midianites were defeated and for as long as
Gideon lived, there was peace in the land of Israel.

A Surprise Haircut

*"If my head is shaved, then my strength will leave me,
and I shall become weak and be like any other man."*
Judges 16:17

Among the Israelites was a very strong young man named Samson. Once, a thousand Philistines tried to kill Samson, but he picked up a big bone and killed them all.

The Philistines wanted to stop Samson. They hated him because of his strength and because of his faith in God. The Philistines asked Delilah to help them. Samson loved and trusted Delilah even though she was a Philistine.

When Delilah asked Samson what made him so strong, he answered her truthfully. "If someone cut my hair, I would not be strong anymore."

That night, after Samson had fallen asleep, Delilah cut his hair. Then the Philistines easily tied Samson up, blinded him, and threw him into prison. But as time passed, Samson's hair grew long again.

When the Philistines later brought Samson to a big feast to mock his weakness, Samson asked a servant to help him put his hands on two pillars that held up the building's roof. Then Samson prayed to God for strength and pushed on the pillars as hard as he could.

The pillars broke and the roof fell in, killing everyone. God had answered Samson's last prayer.

God Speaks to the Boy Samuel

And the LORD came and stood, calling
as at other times, "Samuel! Samuel!"
1 Samuel 3:10

Year after year, a woman named Hannah prayed for a child. When she finally had a baby boy, Hannah was very happy. She named the child Samuel and promised God that Samuel would always serve Him.

While Samuel was still very young, Hannah took him to live at the temple. A priest named Eli became his teacher.

One night in the temple, Samuel woke up because he heard someone calling his name. He ran to Eli and said, "Here I am."

"I did not call you," Eli replied. "Go back to bed."

This happened three times. Finally, Eli realized that it was God who was calling him. Eli told Samuel to answer God and listen carefully to what God had to say.

Later that night God called again. "Samuel, Samuel," He said.

Samuel answered, "Here I am, Lord."

God told Samuel that He had chosen him as a prophet. Over the years, God told Samuel many things, all of which came true. As he grew older, Samuel kept listening to God, and people trusted him.

David Fights a Giant

*So David prevailed over the Philistine with a sling and with a stone,
and struck the Philistine and killed him.*

1 Samuel 17:50

In the time of King Saul, the Philistines attacked the Israelites. The armies fought for many weeks and no end was in sight. Then a giant Philistine soldier named Goliath dared any Israelite soldier to fight with him.

"If he kills me," said Goliath, "Israel wins. If I kill him, the Philistines win." But Goliath was so big, no Israelite soldier dared to fight him.

A young shepherd named David heard about
Goliath's dare and told King Saul, "I will fight him."

"You are much too young," said the king.

"God has helped me kill the lion and the bear who
attack the sheep," David said. "He will help me now."
The king granted him permission.

David went to a brook and picked up five smooth stones. Then he ran to meet Goliath.

When Goliath saw that David was only a boy, he made fun of David. "I will feed you to the birds," he called.

"You think you can kill me with your sword or spear," said David. "But God will help me kill you."

Then David took a stone from his bag, placed it in his slingshot, and aimed it at the giant. The stone hit Goliath's forehead, and he fell down dead.

When the Israelites saw Goliath fall, they cheered loudly and chased the Philistine army out of Israel. With the help of God, they won.

A Shepherd's Song

The LORD is my shepherd; I shall not want.
Psalm 23:1

The children of Israel often sang when they worshiped God. They sang to remember happy times. They sang to comfort each other in times of trouble. They sang songs telling of God's greatness, and they sang songs of prayer asking for God's help.

The children of Israel put all their songs together in a book called the "Psalms." We still read, sing, and pray the psalms today.

Many of the psalms were written by David, who became a great king of Israel. But before he was a king, David was a simple shepherd. He liked to sing to God while he was tending his sheep. One of his songs is Psalm 23.

"The Lord is my shepherd; I shall not want. He makes me lie down in green pastures. He leads me beside still waters. He restores my soul. He leads me in paths of righteousness for His name's sake.

"Even though I walk through the valley of the shadow of death, I will fear no evil, for You are with me; Your rod and Your staff, they comfort me.

"You prepare a table before me in the presence of my enemies; You anoint my head with oil; my cup overflows.

"Surely goodness and mercy shall follow me all the days of my life, and I shall dwell in the house of the LORD forever."

A Wise King

Then the king answered and said, "Give the living child to the first woman, and by no means put him to death; she is his mother."
1 Kings 3:27

David's son, Solomon, ruled after him as king of Israel. God made Solomon very wise. From far and near, people came to seek his advice.

Once, two women came to King Solomon's court. Each one claimed to be the mother of a baby boy. They were angry and argued loudly before the king.

When they finished speaking, Solomon asked that a sword be brought to him. "Cut the baby in two," he ordered, "and give half of the baby to one woman and half to the other."

When he said this, one of the two women cried out
in horror, "No! No, don't do that! Let the baby be given
to the other woman. I do not want my child killed."

But the other woman replied, "No, let the baby be
neither yours nor mine. It is only fair to divide it."

Solomon knew then that the woman who did not want the baby harmed was the real mother. "Do not kill the child," he said, "but give it to this good woman. She is the baby's mother."

When the people heard about the king's decision, they knew that Solomon had truly been blessed with the wisdom of God.

A Mountaintop House for God

*Now Solomon purposed to build a temple for
the name of the LORD, and a royal palace for himself.*
2 Chronicles 2:1

When King Solomon's father, David, had been king, he had started gathering supplies to build a magnificent temple where his people could worship God. But God had told David not to build the temple. David was a soldier, and God wanted His temple to be built by a man of peace. So God told David that his son Solomon would build the temple.

Now that Solomon was king, he decided to finish his father's work. He hired many men. They carried logs and gold and silver up the mountain. It took seven years to build the great temple.

Finally it was ready. It was the most beautiful building anyone had ever seen. The priests brought the ark of the covenant, which held the Ten Commandments, into the most holy place in the temple. This was where God revealed Himself to His people.

God was pleased with the temple that Solomon
had built. He sent His Spirit to enter the building so all
the people could see that it was His house.

The people were glad. They sang and danced and
worshiped God in His temple. Solomon was pleased
with the temple too. He was happy that he had done
as God had said.

God's Prophet Elijah

[Elijah said,] "How long will you go limping between two different opinions?
If the LORD is God, follow Him; but if Baal, then follow him."
1 Kings 18:21

$\mathcal{M}$any years after King Solomon, a wicked king
named Ahab and his wife, Jezebel, ruled over Israel.
They made false gods out of stone and metal and
prayed to them. God sent His prophet Elijah to warn
King Ahab that what he was doing was wrong.

"You have displeased God," Elijah told the king.
"There will be no rain in Israel until I say so."

This made the king very angry, and Elijah was afraid. God told Elijah to hide in the wilderness near a brook where God took care of him. Every day ravens brought Elijah bread and meat to eat.

But there was no rain, and before long the brook dried up. God then told Elijah to go live with a poor widow and her son. She had only a little bit of food left.

"Share your bread with me," said Elijah. "God will give you all the food you need until it rains."

Elijah stayed safely in the widow's house for three years. Then God told him to go see King Ahab again.

So Elijah went back to King Ahab. "You must choose between the false god Baal and the Lord our God," he said. "It will not rain until you do."

Elijah also told Ahab to call all the prophets of Baal to the top of Mount Carmel. The people of Israel came, too.

"Let us have a contest," Elijah said. "Let Baal's prophets build an altar and place dry wood and meat on it for an offering. But do not light the fire. I will do the same thing. Then let Baal's prophets pray to Baal, and I will pray to God. The god who sends fire is the true God."

The people thought this was a good test.

The prophets of Baal prayed and shouted and danced around their altar all day long, but nothing happened.

Then Elijah called the people to come close and watch. He made an altar and put the dry wood and meat upon it. Then he dug a trench around it. Last of all, he had the people pour water over the altar.

They poured so much water that it soaked the wood and filled the trench around the altar. Then Elijah prayed to God.

In a flash, fire came down from the sky. It burned up everything, even the water in the trench.

The people fell to the ground. "The Lord is God," they all shouted.

"God will now send rain," said Elijah. Before long it began raining, and the great drought came to an end. God heard Elijah's prayers and answered them. God also hears and answers our prayers in Jesus' name.

The Prophet's Cloak

*And he took up the cloak of Elijah that had fallen from him
and went back and stood on the bank of the Jordan.*
2 Kings 2:13

The time had come for Elijah the prophet to go to heaven. On that day he and his friend Elisha went walking by the River Jordan.

Soon they decided to cross the river. So Elijah took off his coat and struck the water with it. At once, the waters parted to make a path. The two men crossed to the other side without even getting their feet wet.

Then Elijah asked Elisha what he might like to have from him.

Elisha replied, "Please let me be a prophet like you are."

"If you see me ascend to heaven," said Elijah, "your request will be granted."

Just then a chariot of fire drawn by fiery horses came down from above. A whirlwind swirled round and round and carried Elijah up to heaven.

    With wonder, Elisha watched his friend ascend to heaven. He picked up Elijah's coat, which had fallen to the ground, and went back to the river. Then Elisha struck the water with the coat. Some water went left, and some went right. Elisha walked across the river on a dry path!

    On the far side of the river, a large group of men stood watching. "You have Elijah's spirit," they said to Elisha. "You are now God's prophet." Elisha's request had been granted.

The Prophet's Warnings

. . . Letting Jeremiah down by ropes.
And there was no water in the cistern, but only mud, and Jeremiah sank in the mud.
Jeremiah 38:6

In a part of Israel called Judah, there lived a man named Jeremiah. God spoke to him and said, "Before you were born, I set you apart to tell people about Me."

"I do not know how to talk to people," answered Jeremiah. "I am too young."

God said, "Say what I tell you to say and you will be all right."

After that, God told Jeremiah what to tell the people about Him. Sometimes they listened, and sometimes they didn't.

He told King Josiah and the people of Judah, "God is upset with you. You do not obey His rules."

So King Josiah made his people live by God's rules and God was pleased.

Later, Zedekiah became king. He wanted his soldiers to fight the Babylonian army, which was attacking Judah. Jeremiah warned the king not to fight.

The king didn't like what Jeremiah said. He tried to silence Jeremiah by putting him into a deep well.

But a palace worker took some ropes and pulled Jeremiah to safety.

After that, King Nebuchadnezzar of Babylon destroyed the city of Jerusalem. His soldiers tore down the temple and carried many of the Israelites off to Babylonia.

Jeremiah tried to comfort the people. He told them about God's promises. "One day, God will bring you back to Jerusalem. He will send you a fair and good king from David's family, and you will love God in a new and better way."

The Handwriting
on the Wall

*Immediately the fingers of a human hand appeared and wrote
on the plaster of the wall of the king's palace.*
Daniel 5:5

Young Daniel was one of the children of Israel
captured and carried off to Babylon. Daniel lived as
a helper in the king's palace and learned many new
ideas, and Daniel always loved God.

Several years later, Belshazzar, the king of Babylon, gave a party. At the party he drank out of the gold and silver cups his father, Nebuchadnezzar, had stolen from God's temple in Jerusalem.

Suddenly a hand appeared in the air and wrote four strange words on the wall: "MENE, MENE, TEKEL, UPHARSIN."

The king was so frightened that his knees knocked. He called all his wise men to tell him what the words meant, but they could not. They told him to call Daniel.

"God sent the hand," Daniel said to the king. "It was wrong to drink out of the cups from God's temple. You are a wicked king, and your rule is about to end."

That very night, King Belshazzar was killed and a new king took over.

Daniel in the Lions' Den

Then the king commanded, and Daniel was brought and cast into the den of lions.
Daniel 6:16

Daniel became an important leader under Darius, the new king of Babylon. This made the other leaders jealous. They wanted to get rid of Daniel. They knew how much Daniel loved God, so they convinced King Darius to make a new law. The law said everyone must pray only to the king.

Daniel knew it was a trick, and he would not pray to the king. Three times a day he stood at his window and prayed to God. The bad men were watching. When they told King Darius, he was very upset because Daniel had broken the law.

That night Daniel was thrown into a den of hungry lions.

Early the next morning, the king ran to the lions' den. "Daniel, has your God saved you?" he called.

"Yes, my God sent an angel to shut the mouths of the lions. He has kept me safe," Daniel replied.

King Darius was pleased. He took Daniel out of the lions' den and had the bad men thrown to the hungry lions instead.

Then the king made a new law. It said, "Everyone in my kingdom must worship Daniel's God. He is the living God!"

Daniel was free to pray to God. Just as God helped Daniel, He wants to help us in everything we do.

Swallowed by a Big Fish

And the LORD appointed a great fish to swallow up Jonah.
And Jonah was in the belly of the fish three days and three nights.
Jonah 1:17

God once spoke to a man named Jonah, saying, "Go to the city of Nineveh and warn its people that if they don't start following My laws, I will punish them."

Jonah did not want to go to Nineveh because the people there were wicked. So he boarded a ship and tried to run away. But God caused a terrible storm. Jonah asked the sailors to throw him into the sea. He thought God was punishing him for running away. A big fish swallowed Jonah and brought him back to land.

God spoke again to Jonah, telling him to go to Nineveh with his message. This time Jonah did as God said.

When he reached the city of Nineveh, Jonah spoke to the king and people. He told them, "God is going to destroy your city because you don't follow His laws." The king and people were very sorry and afraid. They promised to be good and obey God.

God was pleased and He forgave them.

Now Jonah was angry. He thought the people of Nineveh didn't deserve to be spared. Jonah made himself a shelter outside the city and waited to see what would happen.

While Jonah waited, God made a tree grow next to him to protect him from the hot sun. Jonah was happy to see the tree.

Then God killed the tree and made the sun hotter than ever. Jonah grew angry again.

"Are you angry because the tree I gave you died?" asked God.

"Yes, very angry," replied Jonah.

God said, "If you are sorry for a little tree, why should not I be sorry for the great city of Nineveh? It has thousands of innocent people living in it!"

At last Jonah understood God's mercy.

The New Testament

The Annunciation

*"Behold, you will conceive in your womb and bear a son,
and you shall call His name Jesus."*
Luke 1:31

$\mathcal{A}$ long time ago, in the small town of Nazareth in Galilee, lived Mary who was pure and good and loved God. God chose Mary to be the mother of Jesus. He sent the angel Gabriel to her who said, "Mary, you will have a baby boy and you will call Him Jesus. The child will be holy. He will be the Son of God."

Mary was filled with joy and answered, "I am the servant of the Lord."

The day arrived when Mary's child was to be born. Joseph, her husband, and Mary were in Bethlehem in Judea to be counted by the Roman governor. All the inns were full, so they had to sleep in a stable. That night, alone with Joseph and the animals in the stable, Mary gave birth to a boy. She called Him Jesus, just as the angel said.

While Jesus lay asleep in a manger, some shepherds arrived. "The angels came and sang to us," they said to Joseph and Mary. "They told us that our Savior had just been born. They showed us where to find the baby." The shepherds praised God and then spread the news that the Savior had been born.

Some months later, Wise Men came. They had traveled a great distance.

"This baby was born to be King of the Jews," they said. "We followed His star from the East; it led us here."

Then they knelt down and worshiped Him. The Wise Men gave Jesus their presents of gold, frankincense, and myrrh.

His Father's Business

"Did you not know that I must be in My Father's house?"
Luke 2:49

When He was twelve years old, Jesus went with His family to visit the temple in Jerusalem. After the visit, His parents and all His family started for home. They had traveled a full day's journey toward Nazareth when Mary and Joseph discovered Jesus was not with them.

Mary and Joseph hurried back to Jerusalem where they spent three days looking for Jesus. Finally they found Him in the temple. He was sitting with the teachers, listening and asking questions. Everyone was surprised by how much He knew about the Scriptures!

"We have been worried," said Mary.

Jesus answered, "Didn't you know that I would be in My Father's house?" His answer puzzled His mother, but she was glad Jesus was safe.

Jesus went back home with His parents. He grew bigger and wiser and became much loved by all who knew Him.

God Is Pleased

And a voice came from heaven,
"You are My beloved Son; with You I am well pleased."
Mark 1:11

John the Baptist was a prophet who lived in the wilderness near Jerusalem. He ate grasshoppers and wild honey. His clothes were made of camel's hair, and he always wore a big leather belt.

John was very wise. Many people came to hear him preach. He baptized them in the Jordan River.

One day, Jesus came and asked John to baptize Him. John did not want to because he knew who Jesus was and that He was holy.

"You should baptize me," he said to Jesus.

But Jesus said it was right for John to baptize Him.

So John baptized Jesus in the river. When Jesus rose out of the water, the sky opened and the Spirit of God, like a dove, came down to Him. At the same time, a voice from heaven said, "You are My own dear Son. I am very pleased with You."

Jesus invites us to be baptized, too. In Baptism, Jesus washes away our sins and makes us God's children.

The Devil at Work

*Then Jesus was led up by the Spirit
into the wilderness to be tempted by the devil.*
Matthew 4:1

After His Baptism, Jesus was sent by God out into a lonely desert for forty days and forty nights. Jesus did not eat or drink. The devil came to Jesus and said, "If You are God's Son, turn these rocks into bread. Then You will have food."

Jesus replied, "It takes more than food to live. Man must obey God's rules."

Then the devil set Jesus on the very top of the temple. "Jump off," the devil said. "God will not let You get hurt."

"It is wrong to test God's love," Jesus answered.

Finally, the devil took Jesus to a tall mountain from which Jesus could see the whole world and all its riches. "If You will bow down and serve me, I will give all this to You," the devil said.

"Get away from Me, devil!" Jesus said. "God is the only one I will worship and obey."

So the devil left Him, and angels came to care for Jesus.

Going Fishing

"Do not be afraid; from now on you will be catching men."
Luke 5:10

One day, Jesus went down to the shore of Lake Galilee. A crowd had gathered to hear Him tell them about God.

Jesus got into the boat of a fisherman named Peter and taught the people who were standing on the shore.

When He finished speaking, Jesus said to Peter, "You, James, John, and I are all going fishing."

"It is useless," Peter answered. "We fished all night and caught nothing. But, if You say so, we'll go."

The fishermen caught so many fish that their nets broke. Fish filled the boats and the weight almost sank them.

The fishermen couldn't believe their eyes. Peter was frightened. The other fishermen were, too.

Jesus said, "Do not be afraid. From now on, instead of bringing fish into your boats, you will help Me bring people into God's kingdom."

The fishermen pulled their boats out of the water and left them on the shore. They left their families and their friends. They left everything to follow Jesus and learn from Him. They became Jesus' apostles.

The Loaves and Fishes

*"There is a boy here who has five barley loaves and two fish,
but what are they for so many?"*
John 6:9

Ⓞne day, thousands of people went out to the countryside
to hear Jesus. It grew late, and Jesus saw that the people
were tired and hungry. So He asked His disciples, "How
can we feed all these people?"

Philip replied, "We do not have enough money to buy
food for everyone."

Just then, Andrew said, "There is a young boy here who has five loaves of barley bread and two small fishes. But that is not enough to feed so many people."

Jesus told His disciples, "Tell the people to sit down."

So everyone sat on the grass. Then Jesus thanked God for the barley bread and handed the loaves to all the people. Then He blessed the fishes and handed them out as well. There was enough food for everyone.

When everyone had eaten as much as they wanted, there was still plenty left over! Then Jesus said to His disciples, "Pick up what remains. Let's not waste even a bit."

They filled twelve baskets with leftover bread! It was a miracle.

Come, Little Children

*"Let the children come to Me; do not hinder them,
for to such belongs the kingdom of God."*
Mark 10:14

Some mothers and fathers heard what Jesus was saying about God's love. They wanted Jesus to bless their children. So they brought their families—boys and girls and even babies—to the place where Jesus was teaching.

The parents made their way through the crowd to bring their children before Jesus. But the disciples tried to stop them. The disciples thought that Jesus should not be bothered by children. He was too busy.

When Jesus saw what was happening, He spoke sternly to His disciples. "Let the little children come to Me, and do not stop them. Unless you love and trust God the way a little child does, you cannot get into God's kingdom."

Then Jesus picked up the children and placed His hand on their heads. He gave His blessing to each and every one of them.

The Little Lost Sheep

"Rejoice with me, for I have found my sheep that was lost."
Luke 15:6

Crowds of thieves and other people who had done
bad things came to hear Jesus talk. The church leaders
and teachers murmured against Jesus and His listeners.
So Jesus told them this story:

"If a shepherd has a big flock of sheep," Jesus said, "and even one sheep is missing, what happens? The shepherd leaves the flock and looks until he finds the one lost sheep.

"When he finds it, he picks up the tired sheep and carries it home.

"Then the shepherd calls to friends and neighbors to celebrate. 'Rejoice with me,' he says. 'I have found my lost sheep.'

"It is like that in heaven," Jesus said. "The angels are happy for the good people who always love God, but they are even happier when a sinner repents and loves God."

The Prodigal Son

The younger son gathered all he had and took a journey into a far country,
and there he squandered his property in reckless living.
Luke 15:13

Jesus told His followers a story: "Once there was a rich man who had two sons. When they grew up, the older son stayed home to help his father. But the younger son wanted to go away and have fun.

"So the father gave this son half his wealth, and the young man spent it all foolishly. He had nothing left. He was so hungry, he took the only job he could find— looking after pigs. He even ate what the pigs ate.

"Then he thought, *Back home, my father's servants are treated far better than I am here. I will go home. Maybe my father will let me be one of his servants.*

"When his father saw him coming, he was so happy, he hurried out to meet his younger son. He told his servants, 'Dress him in new clothes. Put a ring on his finger and shoes on his feet.' That night the father gave a party for him.

"The older brother was angry. 'It isn't fair,' he complained. 'I have obeyed you all these years, but you never gave a party for me.'

"'My son,' his father replied, 'your brother was lost and now he is found. Don't be angry. Let's all be glad.'

"God is like that father," Jesus said. "He rejoices when someone returns to Him."

Make Way for the King

The large crowd…took branches of palm trees and went out to meet Him,
crying out: "Hosanna! Blessed is He who comes in the name of the Lord."
John 12:12–13

It was Passover! Everyone who could went to
Jerusalem for the celebration.

Jesus got ready to go, too. He asked His apostles to
get a donkey for Him and told them just where to find it.

"Untie it and bring it to me. Tell anyone who asks
what you are doing that the Master needs it," Jesus said.

The apostles did as He asked. Then they laid their coats on the young donkey's back, and Jesus got on it.

Their trip to the city was exciting. People laid palm branches in Jesus' path. Some even spread their coats on the road for the donkey to walk on.

"Hosanna! Praise God!" they shouted. "Blessed is He who comes in the name of the Lord! Hosanna in the highest!"

In Jerusalem, Jesus went to the temple. There He found money changers and animal sellers cheating the people who came to worship God. Jesus overturned their money tables. He let their animals and birds go free.

"God's house is for praying to God," Jesus cried.
"You have made it a place of thieves."

After that, Jesus came to the temple every day to
teach. The leaders did not like this. But the people were
eager to learn from Jesus.

A Last Meal

And when the hour came, He reclined at table, and the apostles with Him.
Luke 22:14

$\mathcal{A}$t Passover, Jesus and His twelve apostles took their places at the table. They were going to celebrate together.

Before the meal, Jesus took a bowl of water and washed and wiped His disciples' feet. "Do you understand why I am doing this?" He asked. They were not sure.

So Jesus told His disciples, "You must love one another as I have loved you. Then everyone will know you are My disciples."

While they were eating, Jesus said, "The one I now hand the bread to is going to turn Me over to My enemies to be killed." He gave the bread to Judas, who took it and left the table. Then, Judas went out into the night.

Then Jesus picked up a piece of bread and broke it. As He passed the pieces, He said, "This is My body, given for you. Whenever you eat it, think of Me."

After that He poured wine into a cup. He gave it to His disciples and said, "This is God's new promise to you, sealed with My blood, shed for you for the forgiveness of sins. Remember Me when you drink it."

This was the first Lord's Supper. Christians continue
to celebrate the Lord's Supper to receive life, salvation,
and forgiveness of sins.

After the meal, Jesus and His apostles sang a hymn
of praise and went out to the Hill of Olives.

God's Will Be Done

"Yet not what I will, but what You will."
Mark 14:36

After the Passover supper, Jesus went into the Garden of Gethsemane, which was on the Hill of Olives. Peter, James, and John were with Him. But Jesus left them and went alone to a big rock to pray. His friends fell asleep.

Kneeling by the rock, Jesus talked with God. "Please, God," He prayed, "I do not want to be killed." But He ended His prayer, "I will do what You want, not what I want."

When He finished His prayer, Jesus woke up His friends. "Let us go," He said. "Everything is settled."

As Jesus and His friends were leaving the garden, Judas and some Roman soldiers stopped them. Judas went up to Jesus and kissed Him. This showed the soldiers who Jesus was. They arrested Jesus and took Him away.

Jesus' friends were all afraid. They ran away. All except Peter who followed Jesus and the soldiers. When anyone asked Peter if he was one of Jesus' followers, he pretended that he didn't know Jesus.

Then the soldiers led Jesus across a yard. As Jesus passed by Peter, He looked him straight in the eye. At that moment a rooster crowed. Peter remembered how Jesus had said, "Before the rooster crows, Peter, you will say you do not know Me."

I have failed Jesus, thought Peter. He was so ashamed of himself that he cried and cried. He was very sad.

Three Crosses
on a Lonely Hill

Then two robbers were crucified with Him, one on the right and one on the left.
Matthew 27:38

Early in the morning, the Roman soldiers brought Jesus to the church leaders.

"Are You the Son of God?" the leaders asked.

"I am," replied Jesus.

"That can't be true!" the men shouted. "You must die for saying such a thing."

So the leaders took Jesus to Pontius Pilate, the Roman governor. Pilate did not think Jesus was guilty of any crime. He asked the crowd what he should do with Jesus.

"Crucify Him," they shouted.

So Pilate ordered that Jesus be killed. Then Pilate washed his hands and said, "Don't blame me for Jesus' death."

The soldiers put a crown of thorns on Jesus' head and made Him wear a purple robe. They made fun of Him and beat Him.

Then the soldiers made Jesus carry a heavy cross through the streets to Calvary Hill. There, they nailed Him and two thieves on crosses.

Jesus looked down from His cross at the people. "Father, forgive them," He prayed. "They know not what they do."

Then He died. Jesus had paid the price for the whole world's sins.

Joseph of Arimathea buried Jesus in a small cave cut into rock on the side of a hill. He rolled a big round rock in front of the tomb to shut it.

Mary Magdalene and another woman named Mary watched while Joseph buried Jesus.

Then Joseph and the two Marys returned to their homes. It had been a very sad day, but there would be happier days to come.

Love Wins

"Do not be afraid, for I know that you seek Jesus who was crucified.
He is not here, for He has risen, as He said."
Matthew 28:5–6

On Sunday morning, several women who were Jesus' followers
went to the place where Jesus was buried. But when they got there,
the big stone had been rolled away and the tomb was empty!

Then they saw an angel who said to them, "Jesus is not here.
He is alive."

The women ran back to tell the wonderful news. The disciples
rushed to the tomb. It was true. Jesus' body was gone! Just as
He had said, Jesus rose from the grave after three days. He had
suffered and died for our sins, and now He lives.

That same Sunday, two of Jesus' apostles were walking along the road to Emmaus. They were talking about Jesus and how He had been killed.

Jesus joined them on the road, but they did not recognize Him. He told them how the prophets had said Jesus would live again.

They asked Him to have supper with them. When He broke the bread, they knew He was Jesus! The two disciples were very happy. They hurried back to Jerusalem to tell the others that Jesus was alive.

Later that same night, the disciples were all together in a locked room. Suddenly, Jesus was there in the room with them! "Peace be with you," He said. "As God sent Me, I am sending you. Tell all the world about God's love." Then He blessed them.

Jesus was on earth for 40 days after He died. During that time, He gave His apostles a special and important job to do: He told them to travel far and wide and teach people about His love. Jesus also told the apostles to baptize people in the name of God—Father, Son, and Spirit.

"But wait to do this until the Holy Spirit comes to you," Jesus told them. Then He rose up to heaven in the clouds.

Fire Dancing Overhead

And divided tongues as of fire appeared to them and rested on each one of them.
Acts 2:3

*O*ne holiday, Jesus' friends all met together. Suddenly they heard a sound like a great rushing wind. The sound filled the whole house.

Next a burning flame came down on the head of each person, and they were all filled with God's Holy Spirit. They began to speak in many languages so people from every country could understand what they were saying.

People heard about this miracle, and soon a big crowd had gathered in front of the house. Peter went outside to tell them that Jesus was the Promised One from God. He had died, but God had made Him alive again.

"We have received God's Spirit," Peter said. "And Jesus can help you receive Him, too."

"What must we do?" the people asked.

"You must tell God you are sorry for whatever wrongs you may have done. Then you must be baptized in Jesus' name. God will forgive your sins and fill you with His Spirit."

Three thousand people were baptized that very day.

New Sight for Saul

And falling to the ground he heard a voice saying to him,
"Saul, Saul, why are you persecuting Me?"
Acts 9:4

$\mathcal{A}$ man named Saul thought Jesus' followers were saying things against God. One day Saul and his friends set out for Damascus to capture some of Jesus' followers and put them in jail.

As they traveled along the road, a bright light flashed like lightning out of the sky. Saul fell to the ground.

"Saul, Saul, why are you trying to harm Me?" a voice called.

"Who are you?" asked Saul.

"I am Jesus," came the answer.

Saul trembled with fear and asked, "What do You want me to do?"

Jesus told him to go on to Damascus and there he would learn what to do next.

When Saul stood up, he found he could not see. His friends led him to Damascus. There, Jesus sent a believer named Ananias to heal Saul's blindness and to baptize him.

Saul, who was later called Paul, was a changed man after that, He spent the rest of his life teaching people about Jesus. Paul wrote many letters that became books of the Bible we read today.

John's Heavenly Vision

I, John…was in the Spirit on the Lord's Day.
Revelation 1:9–10

John, who was an apostle, told other people about Jesus. The leaders did not like this, and John was sent away to the island of Patmos. One day, when he was old and full of God's Spirit, John had a vision.

In this vision, John saw God sitting on a great throne in heaven. Twenty-four holy people dressed in white robes, with golden crowns on their heads, sat praising God. In the center was a lamb that had, like Jesus, been killed. Thousands of angels came to sing their praises to God and the Lamb.

John also saw a beautiful city coming down from heaven to take the place of Jerusalem. The streets of this new city were paved with gold, and its gates were made of precious pearls.

A loud voice from the throne said to John, "God will live with the people in this city. Its gates will always be open and everyone will be happy."

Then Jesus spoke and said, "I am coming soon."

And John was glad that Jesus would be coming again. He said, "Amen! Come, Lord Jesus."